Dialogue Productions
in association with
the Yvonne Arnaud Theatre, Guildford,
and The Bush Theatre
present

# Land of the Dead

and

# Helter Skelter

**by Neil LaBute**

10 January – 16 February 2008

# Cast

**LAND OF THE DEAD**

| | |
|---|---|
| Man | **John Kirk** |
| Woman | **Ruth Gemmell** |

**HELTER SKELTER**

| | |
|---|---|
| Woman | **Ruth Gemmell** |
| Man | **Patrick Driver** |

| | |
|---|---|
| Writer | **Neil LaBute** |
| Director | **Patricia Benecke** |
| Designer | **Sara Perks** |
| Lighting Designer | **John Harris** |
| Music | **Nikola Kodjabashia** |
| Assistant Director | **Susannah Pack** |
| Production and Stage Manager | **Sarah Gentle** |
| Voice Coach | **Sarah Stephenson** |
| ASM | **Rebecca Raggett** |
| Production Photographer | **Nobby Clark** |

*Land of the Dead* and *Helter Skelter* were premiered in the UK by Dialogue Productions in association with Guildford's Yvonne Arnaud Theatre and The Bush Theatre.

This production of *Land of the Dead* and *Helter Skelter* is dedicated to Birte and Charlie Schrein.

It is supported by The National Lottery through Awards for All and sponsored by Perspex Distribution Ltd/Lucite, Eos Airlines and the Draycott Hotel.

Dialogue Productions would sincerely like to thank: Neil LaBute, Brian Kirk, Josie Rourke, Fiona Clark and everyone at the Bush Theatre, Susannah Pack, Neil Webb, Ashleigh Hooke, Vicki Fitzgerald, Keith Piggot and Karla Schon, Paula Hawes, Susan Grange-Bennett, Stephanie Gräve, Saka Matsushita, Richard Lee, Robert Merry, Tina Temple-Morris, Eva Koch-Schulte, Janet Gordon, David Harradine, Peter Doran, Yoni Jacobs, Alisdair McGregor, Nadja Reutermann at Espacio and an anonymous benefactor.

### John Kirk Man

Theatre includes *Love And Money* (Royal Exchange and Young Vic), *The Mushroom Pickers* (Theatrepublik), *Abigail's Party* (Pilot Theatre Company), *Butterfly Fingers* (Menagerie), *Changed So Much I Don't Know You* (Menagerie), *My Dad's a Birdman* (Young Vic), *Mariana Pineda* (The Gate) and *Of Mice & Men* (Bolton Octagan Theatre).

TV includes *Angel Cake* (BBC / Celador), *Live Girls* (BBC / Celador), *The Bill* (Talkback Thames), *Extras* (BBC/HBO), *Casualty at Holby* (BBC), *Doctors* (BBC) and *Spine Chillers* (BBC).

Film: *Mrs Ratcliffe's Revolution* (Assassin Films)

### Ruth Gemmell Woman

Theatre includes *Coram Boy* (National Theatre), *Macbeth* (RSC and Albery), *King Lear* (RSC and Albery), *Midwinter* (RSC and Soho Theatre), *Trip's Cinch* (Southwark Playhouse), *Kick for Touch* (Crucible Studio), *Ancient Lights* (Hampstead Theatre), *The Weir* (Royal Court), *Nabokov's Gloves* (Hampstead Theatre) and *Turn of the Screw* (The Queen's Theatre).

TV includes *Poirot* (Granada), *Summer Hill* (Tiger Aspect), *Waking the Dead* (BBC), *5 Days* (BBC), *Silent Witness* (BBC), *Frost* (BBC), *Midsomer Murders* (Bentley Productions), *Tracy Beaker Film* (BBC), *The Bill* (BBC), *Spooks 2* (Kudos), *Murder in Mind* (BBC), *Inspector Lynley Mysteries* (BBC), *Dalziel and Pascoe* (BBC), *Holby City* (BBC) and *Macbeth* (Granada).

Film includes *Good* (Good Films), *January 2nd* (January Films), and *Fever Pitch* (Channel 4 Films).

### Patrick Driver Man

Theatre includes *Othello* (Salisbury Playhouse), *Reverence - A Tale of Abelard & Heloise* (Southwark Playhouse), *Ma Rainey's Black Bottom, London Assurance, Volpone* (Royal Exchange Manchester), *No, It Was You* (Arcola Theatre), *Highs and Lows* (Hackney Empire), *Hunger, Imperfect Librarian, Theatre Dream, Half Machine,* the award-winning *Icarus Falling* and *Poseidon* (Primitive Science), *Christie in Love* (Edinburgh Festival), *Twelfth Night, The Old Curiosity Shop,* (Forest Forge), *Sleuth* (Eye Theatre), *Blondel* (St. Alban's Arena), *Pericles* (tour). Patrick also worked for two years with the performance group OPTIK.

As joint Artistic Director of Dialogue Productions, he has co-produced, co-translated and appeared in *The MC of a Striptease Act Doesn't Give Up* (Edinburgh & Kilkenny Festivals, UK, US & European tours), *Top Dogs* (Southwark Playhouse &

UK tour), *Heroes Like Us* (Edinburgh Festival), *Merlin* (Riverside Studios) and was assistant director on their production of *Monsieur Ibrahim and The Flowers of the Qur'an* (Bush Theatre, Edinburgh and tour).

Television includes *The Whistleblowers, Holby City, The Office, The Last Chancers, Worst Week of My Life, Peepshow, Grass, The Bill, Doctors, People Like Us, My Hero, Ghosts* and *Mr Charity.*

## Neil LaBute  Writer

Neil LaBute received his Master of Fine Arts degree in dramatic writing from New York University and was the recipient of a literary fellowship to study at the Royal Court Theatre.

Films include: *In the Company of Men* (New York Critics' Circle Award for Best First Feature, Filmmakers' Trophy at the Sundance Film Festival), *Your Friends and Neighbors, Nurse Betty, Possession,* and *The Shape of Things,* a film adaptation of his play by the same title. His latest film *Wicker Man,* starring Nicolas Cage, was released in September 2006.

Plays include: *bash: latter-day plays,* written by LaBute and staged in New York in 1999 and London in 2000, both directed by Joe Mantello; *The Shape of Things* which LaBute wrote and directed for London and New York in 2001; *The Distance From Here,* written by LaBute, which ran at the Almeida Theater in London in spring 2002 (directed by David Leveaux) and in New York in spring 2004 (directed by Michael Greif); and *The Mercy Seat,* written and directed by LaBute in New York in fall 2002. In spring 2004, the MCC Theater performed five of his one-act plays, collectively titled *Autobahn.* MCC staged LaBute's play *Fat Pig,* directed by Jo Bonney, in fall 2004. In spring 2005, his play *This Is How It Goes* premiered at New York's Public Theater, directed by George C. Wolfe. In May of that year, the play debuted at The Donmar Warehouse in London, directed by Moises Kauffman. Also in May 2005, LaBute's play *Some Girl(s)* premiered on London's West End, directed by David Grindley. In November 2005, he directed the premiere of his one-man, one-act play *Wrecks* in Cork, Ireland. In May 2006, *Some Girl(s)* had its New York debut at the Lucille Lortel theater. MCC Theater staged and Jo Bonney directed. In October 2006, LaBute once again directed *Wrecks,* this time for the New York premiere at the Public Theater. In June of 2007, MCC premiered his latest play, *In a Dark Dark House,* directed by Carolyn Cantor.

LaBute is the author of several fictional pieces that have been published in *The New Yorker, The New York Times, Harper's Bazaar,* and *Playboy* among others. A collection of his short stories, *Seconds of Pleasure,* was published by Grove/Atlantic in October 2004 and by Faber and Faber in the UK.

## Patricia Benecke  Director

Patricia is joint Artistic Director of Dialogue Productions. For them she has co-translated, co-produced and directed *Monsieur Ibrahim and the Flowers of the Qur'an, Top Dogs, Merlin, Heroes Like Us* and *The MC of a Striptease Act Doesn't Give Up.* Her next work for the company is *Wedding Day at the Cro-Magnons* at Soho Theatre.

Patricia works as a director in the UK and Germany. Previous repertory work includes *Miss Julie* (Mercury Theatre), *By the Bog of Cats* (Heilbronn Rep), *Shining City* (Dortmund Rep) and *Realism* (Bonn Rep). Future work includes

*A Midsummer Night's Dream* (Potsdam Rep), *Woman and Scarecrow* (Dortmund) and *The Hypochondriac* (Bonn).

She is associate director at the Horizont Theatre, Cologne, where her directing work includes: *Ghosts, Twilight of the Golds, The Fireraisers, The Transformed Comedian* and *Far Away* (nominated for the Cologne Theatre Award).

Patricia is also a translator and the British theatre correspondent for Theater Heute and Neue Zürcher Zeitung.

## Sara Perks  Designer

Sara trained at Bristol Old Vic Theatre School and University of Kent.

Recent theatre includes *Treasure Island* (Derby Playhouse), *Rough For Theatre 1 & 2* (Arts Theatre, London), *Coriolanus* and *Julius Caesar* (Mercury, Colchester), *Dead Funny* (Oldham Coliseum and touring), *Return To The Forbidden Planet* (National tour from Basingstoke Theatre Royal), *Singin' In The Rain* (The Courtyard, Hereford), *Arabian Nights* (The Speigel Tent, Oxford), *Hamlet* and *The Merchant of Venice* (site specific at Oxford Castle), *The Crypt Project* (Wren church, St Andrews, Holborn Circus), *Death of A Salesman, Miss Julie, A Midsummer Night's Dream, The Importance of Being Earnest* (all at the Mercury, Colchester), *Be My Baby* (The Dukes, Lancaster), *The Deep Blue Sea* (The Northcott, Exeter). Current projects include *Wedding day at The Cro-Magnons*, also directed by Patricia Benecke (Soho Theatre), and *Journey's End* (Mercury, Colchester).

She has been the recipient of the BBC Vision Design: Costume, the John Elvery Theatre Design Award and an Edinburgh Fringe First award, and has worked extensively in an Associate capacity for English Touring Theatre in the past on many shows including *Honeymoon Suite* (Royal Court), *John Gabriel Borkman* (National Tour), *King Lear* (national tour and West End), and *The York Realist* (national tour and West End).

## John Harris  Lighting Designer

John was Chief Electrician at the Shaftsbury Theatre until 1995.

Theatre includes *Son of Man* (RSC), *Uncle Vanya* (Albery Theatre), *Michael Feinstein* (Comedy Theatre), *Women on The Verge of HRT* (UK Tour),*Small Change* and *Moving Susan* (Basingstoke Haymarket), *Henry V, Macbeth, A Midsummer Nights Dream* and *Much Ado About Nothing* (Arundel Festival) and *Monsieur Ibrahim and the Flowers of The Qur'an* (Bush Theatre). He has worked extensively for the Orange Tree in Richmond where his recent lighting designs include *Myth Propaganda and Disaster in Nazi Germany and Contemporary America, Three in the Back Two in the Head, The Linden Tree, Larkin With Women, Tosca's Kiss, The Madras House, Major Barbara* and *The Pirates of Penzance, Diana of Dobson's, The Years Between* and *Chains*. For Guildford's Yvonne Arnaud Theatre he has designed *The Curious Quest for the Sandman's Sand, Skool & Crossbones, Shake Ripple & Roll, Pandemonium! (a Greek Myth-adventure)* including a run at the Edinburgh Festival 2001 and each pantomime since 2001. He has also relit many shows on tour including *Hayfever, Calamity Jane, Martin Guerre, Dame Edna, Kill a Mockingbird, Month in the Country, Uncle Vanya* and *Mansfield Park*.

As a Vari-Lite programmer and crew chief he has worked around the world including Saudi Arabia, the Caribbean, Paris, Rome, Vienna, Athens and Dubai, as well as in the UK on *Passion Play* (Donmar Warehouse and Comedy Theatre), *Hotstuff* (Leicester Haymarket), *Godspell* for David Pugh, the closing performance of *Cats* (London) for Cameron Mackintosh and as UK Moving Light Programmer for *The Producers* (Theatre Royal Drury Lane).

## Nikola Kodjabashia  Music

Nikola is Lecturer in Creative Music Technology & Music Composition for Media at DeepBlueSound Studios and Campus for Plymouth City College.

Theatre includes *Monsieur Ibrahim and the Flowers of the Qu'ran* (Bush Theatre), *Hecuba* (Donmar Warehouse), *The Birds* (National Theatre), and *The Bacchae* (National Theatre and tour).

TV work includes *Racism, A History* (BBC4) and *Saints* (BBC/ARENA).

Film includes *Green Pages* (Orev), *The Great Water* (Ivo Trajkov), and *Remain Upstanding* (Kristijan Risteski).

He has been nominated for the Arts Foundation Award and won the Public's award for the best new piece at the Moscow Autumn Festival (1996).

## Susannah Pack  Assistant Director

Theatre includes as director, *Ca$h in Christ* (World Premiere, Assembly Rooms, Edinburgh), *Best Friends* (UK Premiere, New End Theatre, Fringe First Nomination at Edinburgh Festival), Hanif Kureishi's *Intimacy* (World Premiere, Assembly Rooms, Edinburgh), Bath Theatre Royal; Bull Theatre, Barnet), *Gathering of Birds* (World Premiere, C Venues, Edinburgh), *My Night With Reg* (MAC, Birmingham; C Venues, Edinburgh) and numerous rehearsed readings, including *Consider This* (Soho Theatre) and *Return, Little Mercury, Return* (Barons Court Theatre). As assistant director: *Underneath The Lintel* (Duchess Theatre), *The Odd Couple* (Assembly Hall, Edinburgh), *Taking Charlie, Oleanna* and *Resolution* (Assembly Rooms, Edinburgh & National Tours). She is Artistic Director of the award-winning company Wisepart Productions, for which she has directed and produced several shows that have toured nationally and internationally. Susannah has been selected for numerous programmes, including the National Theatre Studio Director's Programme and the TIF Producer's Course.

## Sarah Stephenson  Voice Coach

Sarah graduated from Central School of Speech and Drama with an MA in Voice Studies. Theatre credits include, *Little Women, Fuente Ovejuna, Roses of Eyam*, (Guildford School of Acting), *Animal Farm, Watership Down* (Oxford School of Drama) and *Outlying Islands* (Ustinov Studio, Theatre Royal Bath). Musical Credits include, *Daydream Believer, Chaplin* and *Bat Boy (*GSA). As well as Voice Teaching Sarah also runs Voice Workshops for Youth Groups and Voice Coaching with Corporate Clients. Future work includes *The Kitchen* by Sir Arnold Wesker at GSA.

# Dialogue Productions  Producer

**Dialogue Productions** was founded in 1996 with the aim of enhancing cultural dialogue between Great Britain and Germany by premiering the best of contemporary German speaking drama in the UK. Subsequent projects have extended the company remit to wider international work.

Key personnel are German director Patricia Benecke and British actor Patrick Driver.

Company patrons are Max Stafford-Clark, Christoph Marthaler and Nadim Sawalha.

## Productions to date

1996 - 2003: Bodo Kirchhoff's *The MC of a Striptease Act Doesn't Give Up*, staged in London, Germany, Holland, Italy, Ireland, USA and at the Edinburgh Festival

1998: Urs Widmer's *Top Dogs*, presented as a site specific performance at The Truman Brewery in Brick Lane

2000: Thomas Brussig's *Heroes like Us*, in association with NXT, at The Edinburgh Festival

2001: Tankred Dorst's *Merlin*, the English premiere of this modern German classic, at the Riverside Studios Mainhouse

2003: *Top Dogs* revival at Southwark Playhouse

2005: *Top Dogs* national tour

2006: *Monsieur Ibrahim and the Flowers of the Qur'an* by Eric-Emmanuel Schmitt at the Bush Theatre, Assembly Rooms (Edinburgh Festival) and on national tour.

Dialogue Productions will stage the British premiere of *Wedding Day at The Cro-Magnons* by Wajdi Mouwad at Soho Theatre in April 2008

Visit www.dialogueproductions.co.uk

## Guildford's Yvonne Arnaud Theatre Producer

The Yvonne Arnaud Theatre is one of the UK's leading producing theatres.

Since 1991 the Yvonne Arnaud Theatre has created 119 productions (including 60 new plays), which have toured to 80 different cities in the United Kingdom, providing 673 weeks of product for other regional theatres. Of the 119 productions, 53 then transferred to London, 32 of which were new plays. Its scenery workshops, in addition to creating sets for the Yvonne Arnaud's stage, have built for Glyndebourne, the Royal Shakespeare Company, Chichester Festival Theatre and most of the country's leading commercial companies.

Director and Chief Executive
**James Barber**

General Manager
**Brian Kirk**

Chief Finance Officer
**Sarah Gatward**

Funding Executive
**Madeleine Coleman**

Operations Manager
**Nick White**

PA to Director
**Dawn Kerry**

Assistant to General Manager
**Carmela Amaddio**

Head of Sales and Marketing
**Dan McWilliam**

**GUILDFORD'S**
YVONNE ARNAUD
**THEATRE**

## The Bush Theatre
### *'One of the most experienced prospectors of raw talent in Europe'*

The Independent

The Bush Theatre is one of the most celebrated new writing theatres in the world. We have an international reputation for discovering, nurturing and producing the best new theatre writers from the widest range of backgrounds, and for presenting their work to the highest possible standards. We look for exciting new voices that tell contemporary stories with wit, style and passion and we champion work that is both provocative and entertaining.

With around 40,000 people enjoying our productions each year, The Bush has produced hundreds of ground-breaking premieres since its inception 34 years ago. The theatre produces up to eight productions of new plays a year, many of them Bush commissions, and hosts guest productions by leading companies and artists from all over the world.

The Bush is widely acclaimed as the seedbed for the best new playwrights, many of whom have gone on to become established names in the entertainment industry, including Steve Thompson, Jack Thorne, Amelia Bullmore, Dennis Kelly, Chloë Moss, David Eldridge, Stephen Poliakoff, Snoo Wilson, Terry Johnson, Kevin Elyot, Doug Lucie, Dusty Hughes, Sharman Macdonald, Billy Roche, Catherine Johnson, Philip Ridley, Richard Cameron, Jonathan Harvey, Conor McPherson, Joe Penhall, Helen Blakeman, Mark O'Rowe and Charlotte Jones. We also champion the introduction of new talent to the industry, whilst continuing to attract major acting and directing talents, including Richard Wilson, Nadim Sawalha, Bob Hoskins, Alan Rickman, Antony Sher, Stephen Rea, Frances Barber, Lindsay Duncan, Brian Cox, Kate Beckinsale, Patricia Hodge, Simon Callow, Alison Steadman, Jim Broadbent, Tim Roth, Jane Horrocks, Mike Leigh, Mike Figgis, Mike Newell, Victoria Wood and Julie Walters.

The Bush has won over one hundred awards, and developed an enviable reputation for touring its acclaimed productions nationally and internationally. Recent tours and transfers include the West End production of *Elling* (2007), the West End transfer and national tour of *Whipping it Up*, a national tour of *Mammals* (2006), an international tour of *After The End* (2005-6), *adrenalin... heart* representing the UK in the Tokyo International Arts Festival (2004), the West End transfer (2002) and national tour of *The Glee Club* (2004), a European tour of *Stitching* (2003) and Off-Broadway transfers of *Howie the Rookie* and *Resident Alien*. Film adaptations include *Beautiful Thing* and *Disco Pigs*.

The Bush Theatre provides a free script reading service, receiving over 1500 scripts through the post every year, and reading them all. This is one small part of a comprehensive **Writers' Development Programme**, which includes workshops, one-to-one dramaturgy, rehearsed readings, research bursaries, masterclasses, residencies and commissions. We have also launched a pilot scheme for an ambitious new education, training and professional development programme, **bushfutures**, providing opportunities for different sectors of the community and professionals to access the expertise of Bush writers, directors, designers, technicians and actors, and to play an active role in influencing the future development of the theatre and its programme.

The Bush Theatre is extremely proud of its reputation for artistic excellence, its friendly atmosphere, and its undisputed role as a major force in shaping the future of British theatre.

**Josie Rourke**
Artistic Director

## At The Bush Theatre

| | |
|---|---|
| Artistic Director | **Josie Rourke** |
| General Manager | **Angela Bond** |
| Literary Manager | **Abigail Gonda** |
| Bushfutures Co-ordinator | **Anthea Williams** |
| Finance Manager | **Dave Smith** |
| Development Manager | **Sophie Hussey** |
| Development Officer | **Sara-Jane Westrop** |
| Chief Technician | **Tom White** |
| Resident Stage Manager | **Christabel Anderson** |
| Administrative Assistant | **Caroline Dyott** |
| Literary Assistant | **Jane Fallowfield** |
| Box Office Supervisor | **Ian Poole** |
| Box Office Assistants | **Sarah Ives, Fabiany de Castro Oliveira, Kirsty Cox** |
| Front of House Duty Managers | **Kellie Batchelor, Adrian Christopher, Abigail Lunb, Glenn Mortimer, Kirstin Smith, Lois Tucker, Alicia Turrell** |
| Duty Technicians | **Tom White, Jason Kirk, Esteban Nunez** |
| Associate Artists | **Tanya Burns, Chloe Emmerson, Richard Jordan, Paul Miller** |
| Pearson Writer in Residence | **Jack Thorne** |
| Press Representative | **Ewan Thomson & Giles Cooper at Borkowski** |
| Marketing | **Ben Jefferies at Spark Arts Marketing** |

The Bush Theatre
Shepherds Bush Green
London W12 8QD

Box Office: 020 7610 4224
www.bushtheatre.co.uk

The Alternative Theatre Company Ltd. (The Bush Theatre)
is a Registered Charity number: 270080
Co. registration number 1221968
VAT no. 228 3168 73

supported by

## Be There At The Beginning

Our work identifying and nurturing writers is only made possible through the generous support of our Patrons and other donors. Thank you to all those who have supported us during the last year.

If you are interested in finding out how to be involved, visit the 'Support Us' section of our website, email development@bushtheatre.co.uk or call 020 7602 3703.

**Lone Star**
Gianni Alen-Buckley
Catherine
& Pierre Lagrange
Princess of Darkness

**Handful of Stars**
Joe Hemani
Sarah Phelps

**Glee Club**
Anonymous
Bill & Judy Bollinger
Jim Broadbent
Clyde Cooper
Sophie Fauchier
Albert & Lynn Fuss
Piers & Melanie Gibson
Tanny Gordon
Adam Kenwright
Jacky Lambert
Curtis Brown Group Ltd
Richard & Elizabeth
Philipps
Alan Rickman
Paul & Jill Ruddock
John & Tita Shakeshaft
June Summerill
The Peter Wolff Theatre
Trust

**Beautiful Thing**
Anonymous
Mrs Oonagh Berry
John Bottrill
Seana Brennan
Alan Brodie
Kate Brooke
David Brooks
Clive Butler
Matthew Byam Shaw
Justin Coldwell
Jeremy Conway
Anna Donald
Alex Gammie
Vivien Goodwin
Sheila Hancock
David Hare
Lucy Heller
Francis & Mary-Lou
Hussey

Bill Keeling
Jeremy & Britta Lloyd
Laurie Marsh
Ligeia Marsh
Michael McCoy
Tim McInnerny
& Annie Gosney
John Michie
David & Anita Miles
Mr & Mrs Philip Mould
John & Jacqui Pearson
Mr & Mrs A Radcliffe
Wendy Rawson
John Reynolds
Caroline Robinson
David Pugh
& Dafydd Rogers
Nadim Sawalha
Barry Serjent
Brian D Smith
Abigail Uden
Barrie & Roxanne Wilson

**Rookies**
Anonymous
Neil Adleman
Tony Allday
Ross Anderson
Pauline Asper
Mr and Mrs Badrichani
Tanya Burns
& Sally Crabb
Constance Byam Shaw
Geraldine Caufield
Nigel Clark
Alan Davidson
Joy Dean
Nina Drucker
Miranda Greig
Sian Hansen
Mr G Hopkinson
Joyce Hytner, ACT IV
Robert Israel
for Gordon & Co.
Peter James
Hardeep Kalsi
Casarotto Ramsay &
Associates Ltd
Robin Kermode
Ray Miles
Mr & Mrs Malcolm Ogden

Julian & Amanda
Platt Radfin
Clare Rich
Mark Roberts
David Robinson
Councillor Minnie Scott
Russell
Martin Shenfield
John Trotter
Loveday Waymouth
Clare Williams
Alison Winter

**Platinum Corporate members**
Anonymous

**Silver**
The Agency (London) Ltd
Peters, Fraser & Dunlop

**Bronze**
Act Productions Ltd
Artists Rights Group
Hat Trick Productions
Orion Management

**Trust and foundation supporters**
The John S Cohen
Foundation
The Earls Court and
Olympia Charitable Trust
The Ernest Cook Trust
Garfield Weston
Foundation
The Girdlers' Company
Charitable Trust
The John Thaw
Foundation
The Kobler Trust
The Martin Bowley
Charitable Trust
The Mercers' Company
The Royal Victoria Hall
Charitable Trust
The Thistle Trust
The Vandervell
Foundation
The Harold Hyam Wingate
Foundation

# bushfutures
## building the theatre of tomorrow...

The Bush Theatre has launched an ambitious new education, training and development programme, **bushfutures**, providing opportunities for different sectors of the community and professionals to access the expertise of Bush writers, directors, designers, technicians and actors, and play an active role in influencing the future development of the theatre and its programme.

## What to look out for:

### Company Mentoring
Advice and support for emerging companies seeking support and expertise from The Bush

### Future Playwrights
Writing courses with Bush writers and staff, culminating in scratch showcase performances

### Bush Activists
A theatre group for 16+ who will study various aspects of theatre with professional practitioners

### Futures Directors
Opportunities for new directors to work with professional directors and engage with The Bush

### Projects in Schools
This season The Bush is working with schools in the area and giving students access to new writing, new writers and professional directors. If you are a teacher or student, please get in touch to see how we can work with your school.

If you'd like to find out more about how to get involved, please email bushfutures@bushtheatre.co.uk or call 020 7602 3703

# Neil LaBute
# Land of the Dead
*and*
# Helter Skelter

*faber and faber*

First published in 2008
by Faber and Faber Limited
3 Queen Square, London WC1N 3AU

Typeset by Country Setting, Kingsdown, Kent CT14 8ES
Printed in the UK by CPI Bookmarque, Croydon, CR0 4TD

*Land of the Dead* was originally published in the USA
in *Wrecks and Other Plays* by Faber and Faber, Inc

A CIP record for this book
is available from the British Library

ISBN 978-0-571-24222-1

2 4 6 8 10 9 7 5 3 1

# A Short Essay on Short Plays

Why do we even bother writing short plays these days? I'm not sure but I keep doing it with an alarming regularity. The difficulty of getting any play staged in these times of cutbacks and readings and workshops is bad enough, but when you plop a thin sheaf of ten or fifteen pages down on the table, most literary managers just laugh at you and usher you unceremoniously out of their office (the only positive karmic element to this is that they usually have shitty, overstuffed offices that I wouldn't want to spend much time in anyway).

Like the rest of my theatrical career, I do this because it's there. It's certainly not to make money or win fans or gain fame; the number of times that one gets a short play produced and the total monies received for those efforts are laughable. No, I return to this form of dramatic writing in the same way climbers return to the most dangerous face of a certain mountain – because it's there. And not just because it's there, but because it looks so damn simple standing on the ground – it's terrifyingly tricky once you're up there, though. The short play is a bitch and a bastard (yes, it can be both) to master. Like short fiction or commercials or music videos, it's a hell of a lot harder than it looks. To tell a fully rounded story within a few pages, with characters and plot and conflict, is no easy thing and this is what draws me back time and again. Whether it's the monologue form or, as is the case with the two pieces collected here, dramatic dialogues between two people, this is no easy thing. Like a long-distance runner who is asked to fill in for a sprinter at the last minute, you find yourself using a whole different set of muscles that you didn't know you had. Each word begins to count enormously in the whole and bits of exposition start to stand out like neon signposts when you find yourself limited to a handful of pages. But it's great exercise and terrifically precise work that is hugely satisfying when you get it right. To achieve the kind of 'unified effect' that Edgar Allan Poe spoke of is indeed a beautiful thing. You can go crazy trying, but hey, that's half the fun of it.

Do these two plays represent me 'getting it right'? Hell if I know; I suppose that's for you to decide. I love the form of *Land of the Dead*, where characters break the fourth wall and directly address the audience. It's the great secret weapon of the theatre, the monologue and its ability to directly confront the viewer, and I adore it. Breaking the fourth wall and reminding the audience that they shouldn't get too comfortable isn't such a bad thing, either. *Helter Skelter* – which was renamed *Things We Said Today* for its initial New York run (thanks due to The Beatles for both titles) – is a more conventional drama from a structural standpoint, but its message is as old as the Greeks. It is a primal scream about injustice and children and lost love and in the hands of the right actors it makes even my hair stand on end (no easy thing for a man born with a curly mane).

Thanks to Birte Schrein, a brilliant German actress, for first bringing 'The Woman' to such vivid life and also to Dana Delany, a brilliant American actress, for so effectively picking up the sword in the initial New York run. Many thanks as well to Kirstin Davis and Paul Rudd for putting *Land of the Dead* through its initial paces.

The plays were not written as companion pieces, but because of the pregnancy theme that runs through both, they work conveniently and eerily well together. *Land of the Dead*, in fact, was written for a benefit a year after 9/11 (a subject that has been suspiciously underwritten about thus far by American writers. Why? Because nobody likes a loser, I suppose, and there's no way to put a positive spin on that one).

It's been a while since I was lucky enough to have my work in front of an English audience and I cherish the moment every time it happens. There is a common love of language that I share with English audiences (on a par only with perhaps the Irish ones that I've enjoyed thus far). From experience I am now confident that there is no place too dark or too wordy for UK theatregoers to follow me to – the main and perhaps only criterion is that the work is good and singular, and above all, necessary. The same qualities I strive for every time I sit down with my little notepad in some corner of a room as I scribble away, watching another 'useless' short play spill out of my pen. So it goes.

Neil LaBute
15 December 2007

# LAND OF THE DEAD

*Land of the Dead* was first presented as part of the 'Brave New World' festival at Town Hall in New York City on 9 September, 2002, performed by Kirstin Davis and Paul Rudd, and directed by Neil LaBute.

The play was revived at Theater Bonn in Bonn on 7 February 2007, performed by Birte Schrein and Andreas Maier, and directed by Jens Kerbel.

*Silence. Darkness.*

*Lights up slowly on a Man and a Woman, seated apart.*

MAN

Wow. What a day . . . I mean, *what* a day, right?

WOMAN

I'll never forget it . . .

MAN

You know, because, it's not . . . That kinda thing doesn't
just come around any ol' time of the week, thank God.
Huh? That's one of those dates that gets in your head and
stays there. Like, ahh . . . ahh . . .

WOMAN

I got up around three that morning, I remember that.
Very clearly. Must've been around, umm . . . well, no later
than 3.15, anyway. Right about then. It was before dawn,
I know that. It was dark out our window and I just
couldn't sleep, what with it still being warm outside, even
so early, it was warm and I was uncomfortable and so
I got up. Maybe 3.30 but no later than that . . . (*Beat.*)
He was still snoring . . .

MAN

I was out cold. That night? I mean, completely zonked.
I'd been out with some of the guys I work with, my
buddies, and so by the time I got home I was staggering,
not ashamed to admit it. We'd closed a big deal that
afternoon and you gotta take a minute, pound the ol'
fists on the chest a bit when something good happens,
right? I always do. Anyway, I slept great . . .

9

WOMAN

I go to my purse and begin to count the money again.
That's stupid to do, I know, I know that, I must've
checked the thing, like, *sixty* times already, but what else
am I gonna do? It's 3.30 in the morning, or four. Something
like that. Whatever. I count it out again. Should be four
hundred dollars. In tens . . .

MAN

She made me go out to an ATM that night! I'm sloshing
around like that drunk guy off *The Andy Griffith Show* –
the hell was his name again? Oscar, or Otis, something
like that, Otis, I think – and I'm tired, I gotta work in the
morning. She's sitting up when I get in, just after
midnight, and she's sitting on the love seat and just
staring at me . . . says I shouldn't have taken any money
from there without telling her – I snagged a few bills out
for the bar – and I need to go back out. So I empty my
wallet, dig through the sock drawer, any place I might've
jammed a spare twenty but it's no good. We're fifty bucks
short. Great. I'm looking at her face and she's not saying
anything and I know not to argue. I just slip my jacket
back on and head down to the corner. There's a Citibank,
like, three blocks over . . .

WOMAN

I was waiting for him to get that money – I didn't care
about his being out that night, partying, that was fine.
Not like it was some big surprise – I just wanted the rest
of the cash. I suppose now, when I think about it, we
could've just written a cheque, but I didn't . . . I wanted
to pay it, bill by bill, counting it out there on the counter,
so I'd remember. So I'd feel it. Feel something.

MAN

Normally I would go with her, no question. Seriously.
We'd talked about it and I promised I would and so,
yeah, under *normal* circumstances I totally would've been

there. Absolutely yes . . . but the boss is all over me this
morning, wants to go to breakfast, he's calling my cell
by six, busting out of his pants he's so happy with our
closing that account that he's not taking 'no' for an
answer . . . I *have* to go. I mean, if you knew the guy, he's
just . . . Anyhow, she understands. Once I explain it, she
completely understands . . .

#### WOMAN

Typical, right? He leaves it up to me . . . but what're you
gonna do? Get into this, like, big *thing* over coffee about
something that is just not gonna change? I guess you
could, some women might, but that's not me. It's not,
and I don't feel the need to make up excuses. He'd just sit
there, anyway, reading *People* magazine and checking his
watch, so forget it . . . At that point we'd decided, we're
doing it, might as well just get it done.

#### MAN

She leaves a little bit before me . . . maybe ten minutes
ahead. This peck on the cheek and she takes off. Leaves
the stupid money on the table! So I'm running downstairs
in my bare feet to catch her . . . believe that?

#### WOMAN

He comes barrelling down the stairs, yelling out my name
and chasing me. For a second, I mean, just a *moment*
there . . . I thought he wanted to talk, change of heart or
something like that. I can recall turning around, standing
by the mailboxes there, this huge smile on my face . . .
then I see the envelope in his hand. He's sort of out of
breath . . .

#### MAN

I hand her the thing and then, you know, like on *impulse*,
I kiss her again because it's, I mean, it feels like the thing
to do . . . and then I go up and have a shower. Watch a
little ESPN before heading out to Applebee's . . .

**WOMAN**

I took the earliest appointment I could . . . 7.30. I thought
that was the best thing, you know, just get it over with.
Take a little time, but I'm still back to work by lunch. Only
have to use up half a personal day that way. (*Beat.*) The
thirty-fourth floor. Sitting in the waiting room of this squat
grey building, I practically have the whole place to myself.
A young girl – a teenager, I'm sure – a few chairs down.
I look around for a magazine to read, something, but no
issues of *People* anywhere. That makes me laugh . . .

**MAN**

Breakfast is pretty decent. I have ham on the bone, and
some sorta eggs. White toast, which is not the most
healthy thing in the world, I know, I know, but hey . . .
a hangover the size of *Delaware* up there above my eyes.
The boss is droning on and on about production and
output and I'm just staring at him, wishing he'd've been
hit by a taxi as he was crossing the street on the way
over, so I could enjoy my food in peace . . . That's a lousy
thing to say, but it's how I'm feeling.

**WOMAN**

They call my name fifteen minutes later . . .

**MAN**

This is around 7.45 or so. I check my watch right about
then . . .

**WOMAN**

I'd already done the forms and everything, so I go right
in. Into one of their rooms there . . .

**MAN**

Food's good but the guy is driving me nuts, talking loud
and this little bit of jelly hanging on his bottom lip as he's
yakking away. I mean, hell, I might as well have gone
with her to the clinic, the way he's carrying on . . . Least I
could've read a *magazine* or something.

#### WOMAN

I'm perched on the edge of the table there, up on the table with that kind of crinkly paper under me . . . and the nurse is saying something. I remember quite clearly: she said, 'I love your hair.' Then, 'I hate your earrings,' which kind of catches me off guard, and, 'There'll be some slight discomfort.' (*Beat.*) I still have the earrings . . .

#### MAN

No, I'm pro-choice, I am . . . She can choose to keep the kid, or she can choose to keep me. It's entirely up to her! (*Laughs.*) That's a joke, actually, I heard that at work . . . kinda funny. Yep. (*Beat.*) But seriously, think about it . . . what's the problem? You do it, it happens, it's over. It really is that simple. Anyway, I've heard that it doesn't hurt that much – and I mean in terms of physical pain – at least no more than a pretty good paper cut. Now, I know, I know, there's a whole 'psychological' thing going on, I know that. But come on . . . we're still talking about, in essence, a *paper cut*! I mean, who hasn't had one of those? (*Beat.*) Hell, I'd do the thing *myself* if I had the right attachment for the Dustbuster, so I'm probably the wrong person to be asking . . .

#### WOMAN

And I don't really feel anything afterward. Nothing . . . They say I can stay there as long as I need, which is nice, I thought. I sleep for a while – I didn't have to, I really don't feel anything at all, that's the truth, but – I do sleep. A little. (*Beat.*) Someone comes in a bit later to check on me, so I get my things together and go up to the front to pay. At the last moment – I mean, I even reached out and snatched back the envelope – I decide to pay by credit card instead, which somehow seems, I don't know, appropriate. I put it on my Diners Club. (*Laughs.*) I'm not kidding, they actually take my card!

## MAN

Besides, we're sending it to a better place, right? Better than this world, anyways . . . Or maybe not. Maybe it is wrong, hell, I dunno. But you gotta believe something. You do, otherwise . . . Not that I wouldn't've taken care of it. Seriously! I can see myself buying toys, changing diapers, stuff like that . . . easily. It would've been nice. Forming that parental bond, going to school plays, I could've done that. Yeah, I would enjoy a child. I know I would . . . (*Beat.*) Of course, all that's easier to say knowing that the little bundle's safely in some incinerator somewhere. Know what I mean? Oh, come on . . . sure you do. (*Beat.*) Anyway, I leave her a message on my way to the office . . .

## WOMAN

I stop on the street there and listen to him, tuck myself into a doorway and listen. I can tell he's just finished his meal because he's kind of sucking at his teeth, not all the time, but every once in a while . . . this kind of sucking sound while it's being recorded. And as he speaks, he just casually tosses this in: 'I tried phoning you earlier, but I couldn't get through . . .'

## MAN

I tried a couple times before I ate, I really did . . . but she's always switching the power thing 'off' on the side there. Drives me nuts!

## WOMAN

He says, ''Cause I was gonna say, I mean, if you wanna, we can go ahead and just keep the thing. Up to you.' (*Beat.*) I stand there for a minute, supporting myself against the metal doorjamb and not able to speak. My mouth opening and closing for a second, and then I say out loud, not *to* anyone but say it aloud . . . 'Too late . . . it's too *late*. I already did it . . .' I have to play it back a few times . . . just to take it all in . . .

MAN

The whole morning just sucks, I mean, you know . . . what
with the way she's acting about the phone afterwards –
it's like, come on, just *take* the call! – plus I'm running
late . . . it's turning out to be a bad, bad day! Wish I
hadn't even got up, honestly, that's exactly how I'm
feeling by the time I snag a taxi. Wish I was still lying
in bed . . .

WOMAN

And I'm OK, it's . . . it's no problem. The only . . .
I shouldn't even bring this up, but . . . (*Beat.*) I keep
hearing that sound. That 'buzzing', you know, from
the . . . I'm still aware of it. (*Listens.*) There . . . can you
hear that? Right there. Listen. Can you? It's . . .

MAN

Anyhow, I get upstairs, over to my cubicle and just kick
back for a second. Take a breath. Look out at the city.

WOMAN

It's beautiful as I'm heading home . . . outside, I mean.
I decide to walk back instead of a cab. Stupid, but I want
to . . . I just need to be lost for a while, on the streets . . .

MAN

And you know, I don't care what's going on in your life –
money troubles, difficulties with your lady, whatever – a
view like this just perks you up. It really does.

WOMAN

Sometimes, as you're moving along, it sounds like a
thousand twangling instruments humming in your ears . . .
and you can let yourself be swallowed up.

MAN

Up here, in these cloud-capped towers, all your worries
and fears and just, you know, bad *stuff* . . . melts into air,
into thin air. The sky's clear as anything. All blue. Makes
you feel, I dunno . . . alive, I guess . . .

*For a moment, the earsplitting sound of jet aircraft.*
*The light over the Man slowly goes out. The Woman*
*removes a cellphone from her purse.*

#### WOMAN
I kept trying his phone after they . . . ringing it, just
ringing it and hoping that he'd pick up, answer it or
something, all night long. For a few days, actually . . .
but he didn't. He never did . . . (*Beat.*) I still have that
message he left me, the one about not going through with
it, about keeping the . . . I have to save it every week or
so, listen again and save it or it'll disappear. It'll just . . .
be gone. So I play it at night sometimes, when I'm lying
there, missing him. Both of them. I'll play the thing . . .

*She presses a button and holds the phone to her ear.*

#### MAN
#### (*in darkness*)
'Hey, it's me . . . Breakfast was OK, not bad . . . Anyway,
I tried you earlier, but, listen . . . I was gonna say, I mean,
if you wanna, we can go ahead and just keep the thing.
Up to you. Or whatever . . . let's just speak later. Call
me if you need to. I was gonna go pick up the Hawaii
pictures from the photo place, I went by, but they don't
open until nine, and I wanna be in a bit early, get a little
paperwork done . . . 'Kay. Buzz me later. Love ya.'

#### WOMAN
It's funny, the stuff you remember . . . Well, not *funny*,
but, you know. Yeah . . . (*Listens.*) There . . . there's that
buzzing again. It's right . . . is that my phone, or . . . ? Do
you hear that? Do you? Listen . . .

*She checks her cellphone again, then looks around,*
*searching.*

*Silence. Darkness.*

# HELTER SKELTER

*Helter Skelter* was first presented at Theater Bonn in Bonn on 7 February 2007, performed by Birte Schrein and Yorck Dippe, and directed by Jennifer Whigham.

The play was revived under the title *Things We Said Today* as part of the short play festival 'Marathon A' at Ensemble Studio Theater in New York City on 31 May 2007, performed by Dana Delany and Victor Slezak, and directed by Andrew McCarthy.

*Silence. Darkness.*

*Man sitting at a table in some chic restaurant, sipping
a drink. After a bit, he checks his watch. Muzak playing.*
  *A Woman arrives, carrying a shitload of packages. The
Man stands and helps her with the stack – we see now
that she is pregnant. Very.*
  *A kiss happens. Nothing amazing, just a peck. She sits.*

                        WOMAN
. . . 'S crazy out there.

                         MAN
I know.

                        WOMAN
I mean, seriously. It's, like, *seriously* crazy on the street
today.

                         MAN
I agree.

                        WOMAN
People shopping.

                         MAN
Right.

                        WOMAN
They'll kill you. They would actually be happy to *kill* you
if it'll help them . . .

                         MAN
I'm sure.

WOMAN
With a spot in line or something. To grab the last . . .
whatever-it-is that they want.

MAN
Or *think* they want . . .

WOMAN
Exactly! It's amazing.

MAN
Uh-huh.

WOMAN
And a little frightening. Christmas.

MAN
Every year . . .

WOMAN
God! It's . . . (*Beat.*) I love it.

*They look at each other and burst out laughing. Ho-ho-ho.*

MAN
I picked up a few items – that video game they want.
(*Beat.*) And you? Anything good?

WOMAN
Oh, you know, a couple things . . . little stuff, for the kids.
My sister. Nothing that's gonna matter two months from
now, but it's a start. (*Beat.*) Imagine if we'd waited until
after the holiday – if we'd come down here the weekend
after Thanksgiving? It'd be, well . . . absolute chaos.

MAN
Oh yeah.

WOMAN
You know? Unreal . . . Already it's, like, so unpleasant, so
out of the realm of how it should be, the delicious fun
that you can remember from your childhood . . .

MAN

Whole thing's been commercialised.

WOMAN

That's right.

MAN

Turned into an advertising circus . . .

WOMAN

Yes. It's . . .

MAN

. . . a shame, really . . .

WOMAN

It absolutely is – and a *sham*! It's both.

MAN

. . . Oh well. (*Laughs.*) What're ya gonna do?

WOMAN

I don't know. Complain?

MAN

I suppose . . .

WOMAN

That's about it. Max out those cards and complain to
someone you love . . .

MAN

So true.

WOMAN

Cosy up with a loved one in a chic little eatery and bitch
about the state of things. It's the way of the world . . .

MAN

I agree. And we can do just that – either here or once we
get back to the hotel . . .

WOMAN

Perfect. (*Beat.*) 'S what we do every year, isn't it?

MAN

Mmm-hmmm.

WOMAN

How many times have we done this? I mean, these little shopping getaways?

MAN

Ohhhh, God . . . at least since we moved. If not that first Christmas than at least by the . . . yes, second one for sure.

WOMAN

That's what I was thinking. At least that long.

MAN

Yep. (*Beat.*) They're fun, right?

*Man takes a gulp of his drink, finishes it. He glances at the Woman and smiles. She returns it.*

You want anything? I could easily do with another one . . .

WOMAN

Sure. Yes. Bloody Mary, maybe? (*Grins.*) I'm kidding . . .

MAN

'Course. (*Grins back.*) So?

WOMAN

. . . Surprise me.

*He stands up to go off and get the order filled. She puts up a hand, stopping him.*

Do you have your phone?

MAN

Hmm?

WOMAN

Your cell . . . do you have it on you?

MAN

I'm . . . sure, yes. It's right . . .

*He starts to feel his jacket, patting the pockets, and to
search. She watches him while removing her own
phone from a purse.*

WOMAN

I ran mine out of battery. (*Smiles.*) You can take satellite
photos with it but it can't hold a charge for more than,
like, twenty minutes!

MAN

. . . That's so true . . .

WOMAN

Did you find it?

MAN

Yeah, it's . . . one of these pockets . . .

WOMAN

I just want to call the sitter. See how the kids're doing . . .

MAN

Lemme see . . . it's . . . I called them earlier, anyway, said
'hi'. They were fine.

WOMAN

. . . Good. (*Waits.*) You don't have it?

MAN

Maybe I . . . did I leave it in the room?

WOMAN

No . . .

MAN

I didn't?

WOMAN

Uh-uh. Impossible . . . I called you before lunch,
remember? *And* you rang the kids.

MAN

Oh, right . . . so . . .

WOMAN

Did you try the inside one? I've seen you put it in there
before . . .

*Man reaches inside his jacket. Feels around. Nothing.*

MAN

Nope.

WOMAN

Huh.

MAN

Can you believe that? Maybe I've . . . Did I leave it
somewhere? In the sporting goods store, or that . . .?
God, I hate this!

WOMAN

It's not in that pocket, right there?

MAN

Hmmm?

WOMAN

There . . . where the bulge is. That one.

MAN

No, it's . . . I checked that one already.

WOMAN

You did?

MAN

Yes, when I first . . .

WOMAN

Just try it again. Please. (*Beat.*) For me.

MAN

Fine, but I . . . (*Feels inside.*) Nothing.

WOMAN

Really?

MAN

No . . . (*He pulls out his wallet.*) See?

WOMAN

Oh, it's your . . . sorry, I thought that shape was your . . .

*The Man is close enough to her – she suddenly reaches over and feels the pocket for herself.*

MAN

What're you doing?

WOMAN

There . . . isn't that it? Right there?

MAN

That's . . .

WOMAN

I can feel it. In the corner.

*The Man reaches in and digs around – makes it look a bit elaborate. He finally retrieves it.*

MAN

Ah, there it is! Got stuck in the fabric.

WOMAN

Was that it?

MAN

Yes. Tucked up in that, you know . . . bit of cloth where the pocket attaches to the . . .

WOMAN

I see. (*Puts her hand out.*) May I?

MAN

Ummm, yeah, lemme just . . . I'm . . .

WOMAN

I can dial it.

MAN

Fine, go ahead, I just wanna . . .

WOMAN

I'll do it.

MAN

Wait, I'd like to make sure . . .

*She gets a hand on the thing as the Man is pulling away – the phone crashes to the ground. Shatters.*

WOMAN

. . . oh.

MAN

Now look what you've done! God . . . (*Picks up the pieces.*) I don't think I can even get this to . . . Why did you have to . . .?

*He struggles with the battery, trying to replace it. She watches him carefully.*

WOMAN

Do you want me to . . .?

MAN

I've got it. *Wait.* (*Fighting it.*) Damn!

WOMAN

What?

MAN

I think the case is . . . I can hear a piece of it rattling around in there. Listen.

*He shakes the thing and it does indeed rattle. She frowns at this.*

###### WOMAN

Well, it's . . . or maybe you can . . .

###### MAN

Maybe it's broken, OK? *Maybe* that's the story . . . my phone got broke.

###### WOMAN

Sorry.

###### MAN

It's . . . doesn't matter.

###### WOMAN

I am sorry. (*Beat.*) Do they have a . . . ?

###### MAN

No, I'm not going to go wandering around the city, looking for a place where they can fix the thing, I'm not doing that . . .

###### WOMAN

. . . I wasn't . . .

###### MAN

Let's just get our stuff together and go back to the hotel. You can call from in there . . .

###### WOMAN

Fine. (*Beat.*) Are you sure you didn't just turn the battery over by mistake? I know that in the past I've . . .

###### MAN

Will you *stop*? Please? I'm sorry, but I do not want this becoming some . . . big . . . thing here, OK? One of those Greek dramas . . .

WOMAN

It won't, I'm just trying to . . . although I don't know
what you've got against a 'big thing' happening . . . if it's
worth it.

MAN

We'll be back in fifteen minutes. Can the kids wait for a
few seconds or do ya have to get on a line *this* instant?
Huh?

WOMAN

. . . I can wait.

MAN

Good.

WOMAN

Yes.

MAN

Thank you.

WOMAN

I'll be happy to wait until we get back. (*Beat.*) If . . .

MAN

What?

WOMAN

I said: if. *If* you do something for me . . .

MAN

Now what?

WOMAN

Give me the phone. Hand it to me, just as it is – in pieces
– and let me have it.

MAN

What're you . . . I don't get your . . .?

WOMAN

I want to fix it, when we're back – I want to put it all
back together and plug it in and then I want to turn it on.
Do you hear me? I want to turn on your phone and
watch it light up and then I want to check the last few
numbers you've dialled. Today . . . (*Beat.*) I'll wait to call
if you'll let me do that – without you touching it.

*The Man stares at her. Speechless. He slowly sits down
in his chair.*

Would you help me with this coat? Seems very hot in
here suddenly . . .

MAN

Of course.

*He hops back to his feet and moves to the Woman –
leaves the phone on the table.*
*She removes each arm from the jacket and then
stands to smooth out her dress – it is long and icy
white. She is wearing pearls with it.*
*As he goes to sit she snatches the cellphone from the
table and pops it into her handbag.*

Don't do that . . . what're you doing?

WOMAN

What I said I'd do – but without your permission.

MAN

Why?

WOMAN

Because . . . I promised myself, just now, that if you
handed it over – your cell – without some . . . *elaborate*
game, then fine. I'd let it go at that . . . but you didn't.
You did not, so . . . (*Beat.*) That's why.

MAN

. . . That doesn't really help me. (*Beat.*) And why're you wearing that *dress*? It seems a little . . . something for shopping . . .

WOMAN

It probably is. (*Beat.*) A little what?

MAN

Ummm . . . 'summery', maybe? Or . . . I dunno. Youthful?

WOMAN

Hmm. Well . . . (*Beat.*) It felt right this morning, when we were getting ready.

MAN

Oh.

WOMAN

You didn't notice it then . . . when you were getting on your slacks and your shirt, it didn't seem 'a little much' then?

MAN

I guess I . . . I didn't realise. No.

WOMAN

You were going in and out of the room . . .

MAN

Yes, I know . . .

WOMAN

. . . back and forth into the other part of the suite, doing things. *Texting.* (*Beat.*) It never struck you as too much then?

MAN

I didn't . . . Sorry, no. Just now is all.

WOMAN

I see. (*Studies him.*) You can sit again if you'd like . . .

MAN

I'm not sure yet.

WOMAN

Really?

MAN

No, I . . . I dunno. You're acting . . . all . . .

*The Man looks around, realises that this is pretty silly,
then sits back down. Checks his watch.*

WOMAN

So?

MAN

What?

WOMAN

Do we have a deal?

MAN

Listen . . . honey . . . we can . . . I can probably get the
thing to work, if you just give me a minute with it. I'm . . .

WOMAN

I know you can. Of course you can.

MAN

So, then, lemme . . . you know. Let me do it back at the
hotel, when we're alone . . .

WOMAN

No, I'd rather do it myself, actually.

MAN

Come on, let's not . . .

WOMAN

That's what I want to do. OK?

MAN

No, it's not, *actually*. It's not OK. I'm actually kind of
sick of this behaviour . . . (*Beat.*) I mean, what're you
doing with all this, huh? Some kind of . . . I dunno . . .

WOMAN

Who do you think it's going to be?

MAN

What? (*Waits.*) Excuse me?

WOMAN

The first number I find there – which'll be the last one,
really, right? The one that comes up first'll be the one
that you called most recently . . .

MAN

. . . Yes, but . . .

WOMAN

I'm curious . . . who?

MAN

It's . . . ummm, lemme think.

WOMAN

Any idea?

MAN

Probably . . . no, not you . . . I was . . .

WOMAN

Got it?

MAN

No, but . . . Oh, I know who it's gonna be – and this
should be nice and embarrassing for you – it's your sister!
That's who.

WOMAN

Really?

MAN

Yes.

WOMAN

And why's that?

MAN

Because . . . sweetie, look around you. OK? It's the
holidays. You're not exactly the easiest person to shop
for . . .

WOMAN

Ahhh.

MAN

Yeah, 'Ahhh.' (*Beat.*) I called her to get some gift ideas
and, and . . . you know, we talked for a bit, I asked her
how things were going at school, that sort of deal. Had
a nice little chat.

WOMAN

I'll bet.

MAN

Now what's that supposed to mean?

WOMAN

Just that. I'll bet you had a nice chat.

MAN

We did.

WOMAN

I'll bet . . .

MAN

Look, I'm . . .

WOMAN

I'll just bet you did.

MAN

Alright, this is getting kind of . . .

WOMAN

What? Tell me.

MAN

I don't know! Silly, I guess.

WOMAN

You think I'm being silly now? Is that what you think?
That I'm . . .

MAN

Yes, I do. A bit.

WOMAN

I'm sorry . . .

MAN

It's fine, it's probably just the . . . you know, being
pregnant and the walking all over the . . . shopping,
right?

WOMAN

Yes, that's true. I walked all over.

MAN

Really?

WOMAN

Yes – much further than I thought I would. Further than I
told you I would.

MAN

You did?

WOMAN

Much. Much, *much* further. (*She starts to tear up.*) Oh
yes . . .

*He starts to move, to stand and go to her, but she
stops him with a word.*

Stay! Sit down and stay right there . . . No. Don't.

MAN

But I'm . . . Honey, you're . . .

WOMAN

How long?

MAN

What?

WOMAN

I'm asking 'how long?' If I hadn't walked past her street,
down past the park and all the way over by the water –
I was thinking about that little cheese shop at the end of
her block, the one that you've always *loved* – if I hadn't
done that and seen you, watched the two of you out there
on her steps . . . the steps *out*side, that lead up into her
house, how long would you say that this has been going
on? Hmmm?

MAN

I'm . . . it's . . . I can't really . . .

WOMAN

Yes, you can! You can find within you the very last decent
thing that might happen in these circumstances, and you
can say to me how long this has been happening.

MAN

. . . No.

WOMAN

Yes, you can.

MAN

But . . . we're . . .

35

WOMAN

It'll hurt less if you just do it – like when they shoot an animal. Quickly helps. (*Beat.*) Go on. *Please.*

MAN

Fine – six years.

WOMAN

. . . years?

MAN

Yes.

WOMAN

Years? Did I hear you correctly? Did you say '*years*'?

MAN

I did, yes. Six.

WOMAN

So . . . since before her divorce? And . . .

MAN

Uh-huh.

WOMAN

Before she left her husband . . . before that time, you two were . . . on her steps there? So to speak . . .

MAN

I s'pose. (*Beat.*) It's been a while now . . .

WOMAN

I see.

MAN

Right before we moved to the new house. Off to the suburbs, I mean . . .

WOMAN

Really?

Around there. I didn't write it down or anything, so
I'm . . . It's a guess.

Got it.

I'm not proud of this.

Well, that's something.

I'm not . . . Listen, I want you to hear me on this, one
thing about this before . . .

Yes?

I dunno, before you go and get all . . . you know, worked
up about it. Or however you do. (*Thinks.*) This is only
one little part of me, the man that I am. *Me.* I'm an OK
guy, basically, and I think you know that fact. You do.
I've always been – this all sounds ridiculous now, but –
I'm a person who loves you, and the kids, too, which
I know that you rationally believe to be a truth as well.
It is, it's true. (*Beat.*) I didn't want this to happen but it
started out as a comforting thing and it just . . . well, it
just grew. The way things do. It took on a life of its own
and I can't say it's wrong or immoral or whatnot because
that would be hurtful to the little good that's come from
it – and some has, if you believe it or not. There have
been times when a few moments of . . . you know . . .
kept me feeling sane. Or normal. Something. So it's not
my place to badmouth it so that I can try and save face
here, with you. I'm sure you feel differently and that's

37

OK, that's expected, but I just want to say that we're not all one thing, right? Good or bad or like that. We're just . . . people, folks who make mistakes, who do good or bad *things* but they aren't really what defines us. (*Beat.*) I see you glaring at me and that look in your eyes and I'm not defending myself, I'm not, I'm really just saying, 'Hey, honey, it's still me. I'm still the guy you married.' I'm very sorry to have hurt you and I don't feel proud of – No, I'm just gonna leave it at that. I'm sorry.

*The Woman has listened to all of this quietly. Taking it in. She waits another beat.*

WOMAN

. . . and is she? Do you have any idea?

MAN

What?

WOMAN

If she's proud of what's happened? My *sister*.

MAN

No, I don't – I mean, we don't really talk about it much, so . . .

WOMAN

No?

MAN

Well . . . yes, obviously we speak, I'm not saying that, but . . . it's mostly, you know. What you saw. There. (*Beat.*) 'S physical.

WOMAN

Right.

MAN

Anyway . . .

WOMAN

Is it at all hard saying something like that, or do you find
that it just spills out of you . . . ? Hmm?

MAN

Look . . . I'm trying to be adult about this.

WOMAN

Why? (*Beat.*) Why now?

MAN

Honey . . .

WOMAN

I don't get that part. When people have done the most
outrageous . . . shit, right? When you go and do this
completely bad and adolescent thing that will hurt so
many people and is just, like, off the charts, out-of-this-
world insane – sure to cause the downfall of an entire . . .
*family* for years to come, how come the urge immediately
afterwards is always to get sensible? Huh?

MAN

I don't know.

WOMAN

Why?

MAN

I'm . . . maybe because it's . . .

WOMAN

Why would that be? (*Beat.*) How come it's never *before* –
just before you lean over and kiss the woman who is
married to a friend of yours and is related by blood to the
woman you're sleeping with . . . the lady that you've
filled up with the seed of your loins . . . (*Pointing at her
belly.*) Do you even see this? What's going on, right here?

MAN

Of course I do . . .

39

WOMAN

Well, that's good. That's the best news I've had all day . . .
(*Smiles.*) And you two never thought about just saying
something to me, or, like, running off to some . . . you
know, *tropical* isle or like that?

MAN

No.

WOMAN

Why not? Why not go for broke with this, since it's
already taken on all these . . . biblical proportions. Why
didn't you go ahead and 'take the cake' with it? Hmmm?!

MAN

I'm not sure . . . (*Beat.*) I did want to, if you must know.
A few years ago.

WOMAN

Really?

MAN

Yes. I even . . . I dunno, drew up the plans for it all – the
itineraries or whatever.

WOMAN

Ahhh. (*Beat.*) Maps?

MAN

Excuse me?

WOMAN

You know . . . the little guidebooks, with the maps
tucked inside. (*Beat.*) I seem to remember some of those
showing up around the house. 'A few years ago.' Was
that a coincidence, or . . . ?

MAN

. . . Yes. I mean, no. (*Beat.*) I bought them.

WOMAN

Perfect.

MAN

But she didn't want to . . . your sister did not want to go through with it, so I put the tickets back on the charge card and I didn't worry about it again . . .

WOMAN

'Tickets.' *Wow.* (*Dazed.*) And why not?

MAN

What do you mean?

WOMAN

My sister. Why didn't she want to leave with you to points unknown? Why ever not?

MAN

I think she . . . No, I know this, actually. For a fact. She didn't want to hurt you.

*The Woman turns and looks at him – they remain in silence for a moment. Suddenly, she bursts out laughing. Really laughing, hysterics.*
*The Man watches for a moment, then looks around. Finally he tries to calm her.*

. . . Honey. Stop. Come on, stop it. Will you please . . . sweetie, stop this. Stop. Stop it! STOP!!

*And, as suddenly as she began, the Woman does stop. It is deathly quiet again.*

You're making a scene . . .

*A last little burst slips out of her mouth – she throws a hand over her lips and stops. Wild-eyed.*

WOMAN

I'm sorry – don't know what came over me.

MAN

It's OK, I understand, but . . . you know.

WOMAN

No, what? What should I know?

MAN

We're . . . this is in public. So . . .

WOMAN

I see. (*Beat.*) Like when I saw you kissing my sister on her porch? Like that kind of 'in public'?

MAN

. . . I guess. Yes.

WOMAN

I see. Just wanted to be clear.

MAN

Fine.

WOMAN

Make sure we're talking the same language here and all that . . .

MAN

'Kay.

WOMAN

. . . because I certainly wouldn't want to cause a misunderstanding between us. To be the one who creates a *rift* in our . . . little lives. God forbid I do that.

MAN

Honey, can we just, please . . . ?

WOMAN

What?

MAN

I dunno. I was just throwing it out there to, you know . . .

maybe get things started. To *jump*start this. Get us out of here . . .

WOMAN

Oh. I see. (*Beat.*) Then, no . . .

MAN

'No' what? (*Beat.*) Alright, this is going nowhere, so . . . look, I think I should . . .

*He clears his throat and leans in closer to his wife. Just so that he can speak a bit more quietly.*

Let's clear the air here, alright? I do not want you to . . . to take this on your shoulders, to carry the burden of this. I don't. (*Tries to smile.*) It's a mess, I'm aware of that, I know it, but it's not what I . . . what I'd wanted for us. *Any* of us. This is one of those things . . . you know when you hear someone say, 'It just happened,' well, that's exactly the case here! Yes, it happened and it's wrong and all that, I realise that part of it. I do. But what're you gonna do, right? I mean, we've very logically and naturally come to this juncture and the more we . . . I don't know what I'm trying to say, but the harder that we work to place blame on somebody's back, the worse off we're all going to be in the end . . . I can feel it. (*Beat.*) We can be civil about this, seems to me, civil and, and understanding and work toward clarity . . . work together for a better tomorrow. I'm just babbling on here, but I think there's some truth in what I'm saying – Tomorrow is another day and you and I are going to learn from all this, to grow and become richer, better people because of it, we really are, and I'm including your sister here . . . adding her into the mix because, believe me, I have spoken about all this with her – at least over the course of these six years that we've – it doesn't matter. No, what's important right now is healing. A sense of love and forgiveness that the children can feel, no

43

matter how much we tell them about this . . . and I vote
for very little, actually, I think complete knowledge now
would do nothing but breed heartache and resentment
and, and, like . . . *fury* for no good reason. (*Beat.*) Honey –
bear with me on this, OK, because I'm just thinking out
loud here, but I feel pretty – listen, we can get through
this. We can. I don't know how exactly or in what
configuration yet, but we'll get through it. Through it
and, you know what? Maybe even on to some better
thing . . . That probably sounds . . . but maybe so. We
might. We could still break through to some richer and
more beautiful place because of what we've done here . . .
your sister and me. (*Beat.*) So, ummm . . . can we go
now? Honey?

WOMAN
No, no . . . this is perfect. Right here. In this restaurant.

MAN
I don't get why . . . are you hungry?

WOMAN
No, I'm not . . . no. I just don't want to be alone with
you. I don't want that, ever again – after that . . . what
you just spewed – so I'm very happy to stay right here . . .

MAN
Well, yeah, but . . . I mean, you can't stay here the rest of
your life. Right? OK, yes, we have some things to work
out . . . to talk about, but . . . we can't . . .

WOMAN
How do you know that? Hmmm?

MAN
I don't know what you're . . . I'm lost.

WOMAN
Why can't I be here for the rest of my life? How can you
be so sure this isn't the last place I'll ever visit?

44

MAN

Because that's . . . it's not . . . you know.

WOMAN

No, I don't. I've realised today that I do not know
anything – *every*thing that I thought I knew or believed
has flown out the window and I'm starting from scratch.
I mean, yes, normally I would meet you in here and
have a drink or dinner and we'd leave at the end, life
goes on . . . but now, after what has happened to me . . .
how do I know this isn't the last place on earth for me?
Or you? How would I really *know*?

MAN

This is . . . Listen, let me get you back to the room and
I'll . . . I'll go home, head up on the train so you can . . .
please . . .

WOMAN

Because you don't want to create a scene, right? That's it,
isn't it?

MAN

No, I just . . .

WOMAN

Tell me the truth. For once – apparently – just say what's
true. (*Beat.*) That's what it is for most people, so . . .

MAN

No . . . I mean, yes, that's true, the idea of us having
some knock-down, drag-out in the middle of this place
isn't my idea of a great day, *obviously*, but no . . . this is
me thinking about you now. And the baby.

WOMAN

Ohhh, right. Yes. Of course. The baby. Our baby. That
I'm carrying . . .

MAN

Yes.

WOMAN

Which, if I'm not mistaken, I had inside me a few hours ago, back when I was down the street from you and watching you put your tongue into my sister's mouth, your hands going up and down her body, across her soft skin – you mean that baby, right? The one right . . . (*Points.*) . . . *here.*

MAN

That one. Yes, I do mean that one. (*Beat.*) So, can we go?

WOMAN

No, I told you already . . . I don't want to be alone with you ever again. That rules out the hotel, even with you leaving for home . . . because I can't fathom standing up and you helping me with my coat and us walking out together – you carrying these packages because you think that somehow that'll *mean* something – and helping get me back to the hotel, upstairs with all the other guests in the elevator, having to feel you pressed up against me since it's crowded and one of those smiles that you do when we're . . . No. That can't be.

*They sit for a moment, waiting for something else to be said – for now there is only silence.*

MAN

. . . I could put you in a cab. What about that? I'll just run out and . . .

WOMAN

No. (*Beat.*) You're thinking logically now and you need to quit that . . .

MAN

Honey . . .

WOMAN

Stop saying that! 'Honey.' (*Beat.*) Now, you've got to stop being so practical . . .

MAN

. . . why don't you let me just . . . ?

WOMAN

No, I said. *No.* (*Beat.*) No . . . cabs or train fares or
calling our lawyers after making it through the holiday
for the kids' sake and all the rest of it. NO!

*She slams the table top with the palms of her hands for
a bit of emphasis. The china rattles. The Man looks
around.*

MAN

Well, what then? I mean, I'm trying to . . .

WOMAN

What? Finish that sentence, please.

MAN

. . . hoping to . . . forget it. Go ahead.

*Another little burst of laughter; she can't control it.*

WOMAN

Sorry.

MAN

It's not funny . . .

WOMAN

No, I agree with you. I so, so agree with you on that. It's
not. At all. Funny.

*Another burst overtakes her; she fights to overcome it.*

Forgive me . . .

MAN

Whatever.

WOMAN

Yes. Whatever. Like the kids say . . . now I understand
what they're getting at.

47

Hmm?

WOMAN

What-*ever* . . . (*Beat.*) You know how I think this should
end? Us?

MAN

. . . how?

WOMAN

Spectacularly. Vividly. *Operatically.*

MAN

What does that mean? (*Changing tone.*) I'm, listen, I feel
terrible about this, that you'd find out the way you did . . .
Can't I just try and make it up to you? I know it might
take a, a, a long . . . but can't I?

WOMAN

Oh no. No, nothing like that. Don't think so plainly now
. . . you've plotted and planned like a military general for
years – *years* – at least help me finish it off with some of
the glory and astonishment that this union of ours
deserves . . . *Please* do that.

MAN

. . . but . . .

WOMAN

We don't think outside the box any more, do you realise
that? Not just you and me, but everybody, that's what
I'm saying . . . The world has come to a stop. We're off
our rockers, completely mad, but we just keep limping
along, acting like it's all OK and nothing out of the
ordinary could be happening . . . happening right under
our very noses! And all we want to do is get on with it,
to, to keep going to work and down to the grocery store
and off on vacation in the summer and that's it, that's

enough for most of us. Each morning we pick up the paper over our cereal and we see . . .

*She stops for a moment, marvelling at this thought. Grins.*

. . . my God, the things that we're witness to! Tsunamis and hatred and atrocities of such magnitude that it takes your breath away . . . really, sucks it right out of your lungs and whisks it away; but you know what fools us, tricks us into thinking that it isn't really happening down the block and in our state and across the ocean? We get used to it always being somebody else. It is *always* some other person who has their legs blown off in the marketplace . . . never you that gets into the auto accident that sends you smashing through the windshield and having to have your face rebuilt, no, it never is . . . Why is that? I don't know. (*Beat.*) So we go along believing that our children will grow up strong and true and that are husbands will be faithful and we plan on dying peacefully in our sleep and that is how we kid ourselves into taking the next step and the next one and each one after that . . . (*Turns to the Man.*) But I don't believe that any more. Those kinds of lies. I believe we're *extraordinary* . . . each one of us, capable of such amazing things and phenomenal heights. I really do. But do we do it? Do we go off and do those things – nail our demands up on the door of a church, making ourselves heard *each* and every day? NO, is the answer . . . no, we don't. Not most of us. The things we say today are forgotten at the second, the very *second* that they slip from our mouths . . . (*Thinking.*) You'd like nothing more than for me to go quietly right now, leave this place and accept a quick divorce and maybe no one at your work would even realise that some change had occurred in your life! I do believe that's what you wish could happen, there in your heart of hearts – and I'm giving you the benefit of the doubt on ownership of that particular organ – but that isn't what's going to happen here. It's not, my dear, no, it's not . . . so get that idea right out of your head. You and I are going to finish off in the most awe-inspiring way and you'll see it on the news tonight and hardly be able to believe that you, yes *you*, were a part of it . . . now, how many people can say that?

> *She sits, waiting for an answer – the Man shrugs.*
> *Quiet. She is about to say something but she catches*
> *herself. A tiny smile.*

As children we do nothing but read all these stories . . . tales of wonder and of myth. *Legends.* And we never question if they're real or imagined – we just simply believe. Medea and Joan of Arc and, and the girls who followed Charles Manson up a hill one fateful night . . . they were all just people at one time . . . like you and me and anyone else. (*Beat.*) And then a thing happens, some *thing* happens inside them or to them . . . they wake up or get pushed off a ledge, a light turns off or on and snap! They are never the same again – and off they go on their merry way. Maybe to wander about the city first . . . block after block after block, trying to imagine that what they saw wasn't really true but they know it is, they *know* it, and that's when they stop and buy a dress, a dress that is perhaps too young for them, yes, far too '*youth*ful', but it reminds them of a time when they were lovely and carefree and of an age before they'd ever-even-heard-your-name – you were right about what I wore out of the hotel this morning, good for you! – and then they make their way over to a restaurant where they know their husband will be waiting for them . . . but that's how it happens to people. People just like me – real and normal and not at all fantastic or anything special . . . this is the *only* way that many of us will ever have the

world turn its weary head toward us one time in our
entire lives. This is how we become . . . *remembered.*

MAN

What're you talking about? Honey . . . sorry, sweetie . . .
I don't get what you're saying.

WOMAN

You don't? Really?

MAN

No . . . I mean, I follow you, some of your ideas there,
but you're not making . . .

WOMAN

Here's what I'm saying – that *this* is how it all begins.
With a single step. (*Beat.*) This . . . is . . . what . . . we . . .
become . . .

*Without warning, the Woman picks up a steak knife off*
*the table and plunges it into her protruding belly. It sticks*
*there, wedged deep inside her flesh. Her eyes grow*
*wider but she remains lucid, even as she screams out.*

AAAAAAAAWWWWWWWWWWWW!!!!!

*Somehow she pulls it out, then slams it back in.*
*Deeper.*
  *The Man is frozen for a moment. When he finally*
*reacts, it is too late – he reaches for the Woman but*
*she is too quick for him; she has scooped up his knife*
*and holds it in her hands.*

MAN

Oh my God . . . oh my God . . . OH MY GOD!!

WOMAN

Now . . . what . . . do . . . you . . . do? Now . . . what?

*The crimson stain is growing on her dress. The Man*
*can't seem to decide what to do. He shuffles back and*
*forth.*

51

OH MY GOD . . . SOMEBODY HELP US . . . HELP US!!

WOMAN

Now what?

MAN

HELP US, PLEASE! SOMEBODY HELP! SOMEBODY!

WOMAN

Now . . .

MAN

HELP! HELP ME!! PLEASE HELP!! PLEASE!!!

WOMAN

. . . what?

*The Woman continues to hold the knife, pointed toward the Man; he finally bolts and runs off. Desperate.*

*The Woman slowly turns out toward us – carefully puts the knife down on the table. Sits back. Hands on her belly. The stain continues to spread.*

*Sound of muzak growing to a roar. Overtaking everything.*

*Silence. Darkness.*